All y… ..

THEY say that if you can reme… …ies you were not there.

In reality, most people were too busy earning a crust, bringing up families and making ends meet, to trog around in psychedelic outfits and challenge the status quo. Yet if you were young, single and tantalised you will certainly remember it was all ‘happening’ in the ‘60s, when colourful clothes and flower power reached their zenith.

Perhaps no other decade has given the country more than those 10 heady years. And much of it came from Liverpool.

The city skyline was changing like no other time and things were looking up. And so were Scousers, to imposing landmarks like St John's Beacon and the Metropolitan Cathedral. Under the river, a new tunnel was being dug that would open the next decade.

The nouveau riche were Ford workers, and the car was king. No pedestrian precincts.

You could drive past George Henry Lee's to a true city centre that had not yet been turned into a bus rank.

There were still great liners in the dry dock at Gladstone. There was also the world's largest floating crane, the Mammoth: capable of lifting 200 tons and boasting the slogan: "If a ship can hold it, Merseyside can load it."

The hardy took the plunge at New Brighton open-air baths. When it snowed you could skate on the canal, more full of ice-entombed iron bedsteads than barges.

At Goodison and Anfield, there were trophy rooms to be filled. Catterick and Shankly assembled sides that will live forever in the memories of every football fan who witnessed them in action.

And in Mathew Street something big was happening. Four lads were about to shake the world. They did.

Words: Vicky Andrews, James Cleary, Peter Grant, Colin Hunt

Photography: Liverpool Daily Post and Echo Archives

Picture Research: Leslie Rawlinson, Brian Johnston

Design and Layout: Matthew Barnes, Zoe Egan, Colin Harrison, Charlie Hearnshaw, Tracy Sucksmith

Published by: Trinity Mirror Merseyside, PO Box 48, Old Hall Street, Liverpool L69 3EB

Printed by: Pensord, Tram Road, Pontllanfraith, Blackwood NP12 2YA

ISBN: 978 -1- 906802 -18 - 9

Smoke billows from the upper floors of Henderson's at Church and Williamson Streets, Liverpool, on Wednesday afternoon, June 22, 1960. This tragic blaze which claimed 11 lives, totally destroyed this famous department store

Making the News 1960

HENDERSON'S UP IN FLAMES

IN 100 horror-packed minutes, 11 people died on June 22, 1960, when flames destroyed the £1m luxury store of William Henderson's in Church Street, Liverpool.

The firefighters' task was hopeless from the start. The alarm was raised at 2.23pm and the fire – believed to have started in the restaurant kitchen – swept through the building with terrifying speed. There was a staff of 500 working for Henderson's – one of the few big Liverpool stores open on a Wednesday afternoon – and hundreds of shoppers and workmen from several firms of building contractors. Reinforcements were ordered from suburban fire stations and Bootle and Lancashire county brigades. Within 30 minutes, 27 appliances, including five turntable ladders, were at the scene and more than 100 firefighters at work. A Liverpool Echo reporter at the time said: "The scene in Church Street resembled the worst days of the Blitz, with smoke belching from the store and a tangled jungle of hoses lying on the road."

Flames leaped 60ft across Williamson Street and set light to the fronts of Jay's furnishing store and Smith's music shop. The roof of nearby Tatlers News Cinema also caught fire from burning embers. Church Street was closed to traffic for nearly three weeks. Henderson's were back in business within six weeks, at temporary premises in Williamson Street.

memorable movies!

NATIONAL HEADLINES

14 March The British radio telescope at Jodrell Bank in Cheshire sets a new space record by making contact with the American Pioneer V satellite at a distance of 407,000 miles.

18 April 60,000 protestors stage a demonstration in London against nuclear weapons.

6 May More than 20 million viewers tune in to watch Princess Margaret and Anthony Armstrong Jones marry at Westminster Abbey, the first ever televised royal wedding service.

21 July Navigator and yachtsman Francis Chichester completes a record solo Atlantic crossing in 40 days on board Gypsy Moth II.

25 August The Summer Olympics in Rome are opened – Great Britain and Ireland win 2 gold, 6 silver and 12 bronze medals at the magnificent event.

30 October The first successful kidney transplant in the UK is performed in Edinburgh by Sir Michael Woodruff and his team.

9 November John Fitzgerald Kennedy is elected as the new president of the United States.

10 November The first uncensored version of Lady Chatterley's Lover – banned for more than 30 years – sells 200,000 copies in one day.

31 December The farthing ceases to be legal tender.

Top of the Pops

Michael Holliday (left) – Starry Eyed
Lonnie Donegan – My Old Man's A Dustman
Everly Brothers – Cathy's Clown
The Shadows – Apache
Elvis Presley – It's Now Or Never

Bumper to bumper: A train-load of Vivas, en route for the docks, leaving Hooton Station, July 1967

Viva la progress

Driving force behind the new Detroit

THE car industry in Liverpool exploded into life in the Sixties.

"The region is on the verge of becoming the Detroit of Great Britain," said the Lord Mayor of Liverpool, Alderman David Cowley, in the Liverpool Echo, on September 24, 1965.

At the beginning of the decade, shadow chancellor Harold Wilson and Jack Braddock, husband of the redoubtable Bessie, were instrumental in bringing Ford to Merseyside.

Halewood, Ford's second largest manufacturing centre in Britain, started in 1960 when Ford bought the land from Liverpool Corporation and the British Transport Commission.

Hundreds of Vivas lined up on the quays at Ellesmere Port, to be loaded aboard La Primavera, 1969

Below: An historic moment as the first Vauxhall Viva rolls off the Ellesmere Port production line, June 1, 1964

While 1,750 workmen raised the Halewood plant from the ground, the first local Ford recruits began training in an aircraft hangar leased at Liverpool Airport.

The plant was officially opened on March 8, 1963. The Lord Mayor of Liverpool drove a lime green Ford Anglia de Luxe, registered IKF, off the end of the assembly line to celebrate the event. The Ford Escort range was introduced at the plant in 1968.

The foundation stone for Vauxhall's Ellesmere Port plant was laid in November, 1962, and the plant was completed in 1968.

It was built on a former airfield called Hooton Park used in both World Wars and the 400-acre site was bought by General Motors from the Ministry of Defence. Manufacturing started in 1962.

On June 1, 1964, the first Viva to be built at the new Ellesmere Port factory left the line.

The cost of the first Viva was £527 (with tax) and £566 for the de Luxe model.

A crossbar ride for a little girl in rush hour traffic in Great Charlotte Street in 1962. St John's Market was in its temporary Clayton Square home

The line-up of fine Bedford fire engines at Bootle's central fire station, 1966

Liverpool's Pier Head in the Atlantean bus era

Pre-Merseyrail commuters from Ormskirk arrive at Exchange Station in August 1964

'Above us only sky' –
Speke Airport in July 1968

Jet set go!

Enjoying flights of fancy

A PIONEER of air travel, Liverpool Airport was still reaching for the skies in the 1960s.

The decade saw the growth of jet passenger craft and Liverpool figured prominently. Regular flyers were the Beatles and Gerry and the Pacemakers, who often had to hide in freight sheds to avoid eager fans besieging the terminal.

In 1960 the Ministry of Aviation returned control of the airport to the council and in 1966 the authorities invested in the main 7,500ft-long runway.

It enabled the airport to stay open for 24 hours a day and handle any aircraft. Traffic passing through Liverpool ranged from engine and plane parts destined for the next ship out of the port, to race horses heading for Aintree and a complete restock of penguins for Chester Zoo!

Many will remember travelling on or spectating from the terminal balconies, the Dakotas, Viscounts and Britannias flown by Starways, British Eagle and Cambrian Airways. Passengers were smartly dressed and 'air rage' was unknown, everyone was just happy to be onboard.

Although rumour has it, there was a good reason why cabin crew got through so many food trays during a Cambrian Airways' rugby club charter.

The De Havilland Dove starts its three day a week service between Liverpool and Bristol, April 4, 1960

The first crew signs in as Liverpool Airport reverts to the city council's control from the Ministry of Aviation in 1961

It may have been raining in Liverpool in July 1962, but the Spanish sun was just a couple of hours away

As one stewardess walked along the aisle, she continuously had her bottom pinched by the cheery supporters on-board.

Being the unreconstructed 1960s, the men didn't realise they were being chauvinistic or sexist, so the crew devised an immediate solution.

A second stewardess followed her colleague and bashed any bottom pincher smartly over the head with a tray.

Swinging into fashion

City is every inch the star of the show

JUST call them the Sexy Swinging Sixties!

Skirts were getting shorter at the rate of one inch a year. And the girls of Liverpool were at the forefront in this fashion revolution.

Youngsters were exposed to a welter of inspirational sources on what to wear. On TV, the Granada Scene at 6.30pm and Ready Steady Go later on Friday evening, featured people handpicked for their cutting-edge style.

When Mary Quant started mass-producing her collections it gave Liverpool girls the chance to try out the new shorter skirts and boots, from trendy boutiques such as Lucinda Byre's on Bold Street.

The Beat look was also fashionable amongst women in Liverpool, with shops selling tight pencil skirts and polo sweaters, perhaps a beret tilted to one side of the head if you were really working the Left Bank look.

Skirts had front and back inverted pleats called kick pleats and were ideal for doing the twist or the 'Cavern Stomp' as they allowed the knees to move freely.

When The Beatles' distinctive take on the Mod suit was beamed up and down the country more lads started asking for it, and suddenly the staff at Eric's couldn't make enough of them.

All the boys from Gerrard Gardens and the Bullring were very fashion conscious and they all suddenly switched to the Mod look.

Every single fella on the West Derby Road wore that same black suit in '64 and '65.

Sharp suits were all you saw round the Grafton, the Locarno, the Aintree Institute, the Orrell Park Ballroom and the later explosion of clubs like Beachcomber and Ugly's.

And when a model or rockstar was looking for the perfect outfit to bring on a flashbulb frenzy they turned to one man – Ossie Clark.

His designs were coveted by the international jet-set and earned him the title "King of the King's Road".

Girl groups, Sixties style. The Three Bells, later The Satin Bells

Above: That 'just got out of bed' look. Liverpool's much-maligned craze of wearing pyjamas in public has a long history

Left: Suited and booted but no fur or feathers – Chick Graham and the Coasters

Twiggy – the world's first supermodel

Short skirts and scooters at the 1960 Motor Cycle Show

Leather and denim, duffle coats and cord, all worn with Scouse attitude. Mathew Street fashion in 1964

1967 and young people celebrate 'The other Southport Flower Show'

THE MAN WHO SHOT THE QUEEN

IN May 1961, Liverpool Echo picture editor Neville Willasey caused a panic during a Royal visit.

The Queen and Prince Philip were attending a Royal gala performance of Snow White and the Seven Dwarfs at Liverpool's Empire Theatre.

Just as the Royal couple were about to go up the steps to the theatre there was a loud bang and a flash. Panic followed and security men thought it was an assassination attempt. Then the truth dawned – Neville's flash bulb had exploded.

The Queen kept her cool and smiled and said: "Goodness, I've just been shot."

Neville was also in a panic — he had lost his picture. But he climbed up the front of the Empire and got a scoop shot through a window of the Royals meeting the cast of the show as they lined up before them. He made page one — so did the report of the incident in most national papers. It was the only time in his 42-year career Neville had made the news instead of recording it.

It was a first for another Liverpool Echo photographer – Stephen Shakeshaft was outside the Empire for the 1961 show as a trainee. He said: "The Queen's limo drew up, she emerged and I held up the camera to my eye.

"She stumbled slightly, so I hesitated before pressing the shutter.

"Then I set the flash off, the Queen smiled straight into the lens and I had a good picture.

"A few days later, I received a message from the lord lieutenant's office. The Queen had commented on the photographer waiting until she composed herself. It wouldn't have happened in London, she said."

memorable movies!

NATIONAL HEADLINES

6 March Lancashire-born 'Ukulele King' George Formby dies after suffering a heart attack, aged 56.

18 April The Soviet Union beats the USA in the race to get the first man into space. Major Yuri Alexeyevich Gagarin was fired from the Baikonur launch pad in Kazakhstan and orbited the Earth for 108 minutes.

1 May Betting shops are legalised following the introduction of the new Betting and Gaming Act. Gambling for small sums, for games of skill such as bridge, is also now legal.

5 May Commander Alan Shepard becomes the first American in space.

21 July The Runcorn Widnes Bridge, to be known later as the Silver Jubilee Bridge, is opened by Princess Alexandra.

13 August Troops in East Germany seal the border between East and West Berlin, shutting off the escape route for thousands of refugees from the East.

4 December Birth control pills for women become available on the National Health Service.

Top of the Pops

Del Shannon - Runaway
Frankie Vaughan (left) – Tower of Strength
John Leyton – Johnny Remember Me
Helen Shapiro – Walkin' Back to Happiness
Danny Williams – Moon River

Day Trippers yeah!

Chasing the sun

DAY-TRIPPING was a popular past time in the '60s. Liverpudlians would pack out the Mersey ferries and the trains.

Children with buckets and spades at the ready were well prepared for a fun trek to the golden sands of New Brighton – the mint rock and deck chair haven.

Their fairground was one of the most vibrant in the north of England.

Some families would even venture out further afield to Southport and Blackpool – tickets to ride. A cheery 'n' cheap escapism.

North Wales was also a regular destination – another world with a strange language and it could all be done in a day. Castles would be invaded by armies of schoolkids in famous places with difficult names to pronounce such as Llandudno and Llangollen.

The latter had its world famous musical festival where you could see a united nations-styled gathering of people in lovely national costumes.

They had countryside in Wales too, where you could see waterfalls and chase countless sheep. Conway Castle was a favourite scene of many a school army battling its way in the souvenir shops for plastic swords.

Closer to home, Chester Zoo was a magical world. Lions, tigers, penguins and did they have Gnus for you . . .

The historic windmill at Bidston Hill had its fair share of visitors curious to see piece of industrial heritage.

And Parkgate too, a unique place where the river went out but never came back.

Liverpudlians loved getting away for the day – even if it meant going to 'Our Gate' – a picnic in Sefton Park where mum and dad could visit the aviary and the kids could fish for tiddlers by the statues of Peter Pan.

And if the pennies simply didn't stretch, a bus ride to the river to watch the ships sail by – a holiday breather in itself. Halcyon away days – memories with a wonderful daze.

Dune adventures and a picnic in Blundellsands, 1966

Chester Zoo, 1960, and Mary has Robert's spade. So Mary decides it is really a cello, despite a painstaking demonstration by Peter

Above: All the fun of the fair at New Brighton

Left: Crowds throng Liverpool landing stage waiting to board the ferry at lunchtime – 1966

Away Days

Above: Swan Lake. Sefton Park in 1967

Left: Lemonade weather for these New Brighton visitors

The height of summer 1960, and hundreds of cars park up on Southport beach

One way of resting tired feet – Southport, June 1960

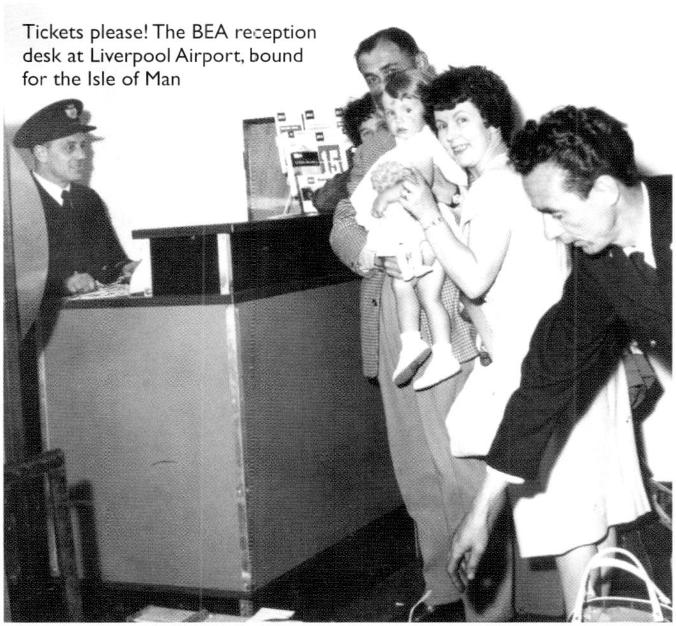

Tickets please! The BEA reception desk at Liverpool Airport, bound for the Isle of Man

Dancing on ice – skaters at The Silver Blades Ice Rink, March 19, 1960

A cold start

In winter's unrelenting grip again and again

'Snow stopping' girls on their way to school, 1966

Right: Floods at Aintree, 1967

THE Swinging Sixties also had a spell of the Shivering Sixties as Merseyside iced up.

In December 1961, more than 15 degrees of frost were recorded at Liverpool Airport – the coldest night since January 1958.

Hardly a county in Britain was free from ice and many had dense fog. In Liverpool, ambulances ferried people to hospital who had collapsed with the cold.

Trains were delayed for many hours. The ice on city ponds was more than three inches thick and the marine lake at West Kirby was frozen solid to a depth of six inches. Plumbers did a roaring trade as cisterns exploded and steam vent pipes became blocked with ice.

The big freeze continued into the New Year and on January 1, 1962, more than 150,000 miles of roads were seriously affected by ice and snow, and at least 40 main roads blocked or impassable.

Road conditions were the worst yet experienced in this country. The slow thaw eventually crept over Merseyside two days later.

The following year, Merseyside and the rest of Britain was in winter's unrelenting grip again. From Land's End to John O'Groats the picture in January, 1963, was of ice-rutted, hard-packed, frozen snow and blocked and ice-bound roads.

North West Coal Board delivery lorries were working seven days a week to meet the rush of orders.

But the Sixties wasn't all grey days and in the summer of 1969, Liverpool was basking in a heatwave. Sunseekers hit the beaches of New Brighton and Southport, while office workers headed to the Pier Head or St John's Gardens to catch some rays on their lunch break.

Weather

Lowry figures in a winter's landscape. Intrepid walkers test the ice on frozen Sefton Park lake in January 1963

When the temperature soars into the eighties some people take to the water, like these bathers at New Brighton open-air baths

Right: An ingenious way of getting from A to B in the snow

Far right: Welly weather at New Brighton, 1967

Making the News

1962

NEW WAVE FOR HOVERMANIA

HOLIDAYMAKERS were floating on air when the world's first passenger Hovercraft launched between Wallasey and Rhyl on July 20, 1962.

Heralded alongside Concorde as the brave new face of travel, hopes were high that Hovermania was the coming thing. The first working model had been produced in 1956 and the first full-size test craft built three years later. This was the transport of the future, enthusiasts believed.

The Hovercoach, as it was called, cruised at 60 knots and was powered by four 400hp gas turbine engines. Floating around on a cushion of air on land or water seemed a rather sedate mode of transport. For just £1 excited passengers could take the 19-mile trip aboard the revolutionary craft across the Dee estuary to Rhyl. Holidaymakers loved it and more than 5,000 seats were sold before the launch date.

The summer service – a joint venture by British United Airways, Vickers Armstrong and BP – was never expected to make a profit. The main aim was to prove the viability of a Hovercraft service and to study costs.

But Hovercraft operations were prone to disruption and cancellation during bad weather and operations became increasingly uneconomic with rising costs for fuel and maintenance. Today the only commercial Hovercraft service in Britain is between Portsmouth and the Isle of Wight. However, there's always the hover lawnmower, a lasting legacy of the technology.

memorable movies!

NATIONAL HEADLINES

Liverpool's first panda crossing, Aigburth Road, Rosslyn Street junction

2 April Panda crossings are introduced in London but cause confusion among both drivers and pedestrians.

11 July The Telstar satellite beams a live television broadcast from the USA to Britain for the first time.

20 July The world's first regular passenger Hovercraft service is introduced between Rhyl and Wallasey.

5 August The last of the love goddesses, Marilyn Monroe, is found dead at her Hollywood home.

28 October The Cuban missile crisis comes to an end, as Russian leader Nikita Khrushchev agrees to dismantle all Russian missiles based in Cuba and ship them back to the Soviet Union.

6 December A choking fog spreads across Britain – the Ministry of Health warns those most at risk, such as those with heart or chest complaints, to stay indoors and rest as much as possible.

22 December Britain's 'Big Freeze' takes a hold, one of the coldest winters on record.

Top of the Pops

Cliff Richard & The Shadows – The Young Ones
Frank Ifield – I Remember You
The Tornados – Telstar
Mike Sarne & Wendy Richard – Come Outside
Elvis Presley (left) – Return to Sender

Happy hours and dancing days

The Pool of life

THEY were the venues in which friendships were made, couples were paired and hearts were broken.

Revellers packed into The Grafton and its sister ballroom The Locarno. The Grafton became known as a venue for the new Mersey Beat bands, and for big visiting acts. Joe Loss, Victor Silvester, Henry Hall, Duke Ellington, The Beatles and the Rolling Stones played there.

At the Stork Hotel, theatregoers would take a nightcap, served by waiters in white jackets and waitresses in frilly caps. The poshest hotel was still The Adelphi.

For those of stouter constitution, there were four Yates's Wine Lodges, and one bar, The Spanish House, which made the Lodges look like health clubs. Red lino and sawdust was the decor. We all did the conga out of there on the night man landed on the moon.

At one time Liverpool was literally awash with pubs. Scotland Road alone contained more pubs than any other in Liverpool.

Young renegades exchanged poetry in Ye Crack, The Phil or The Jac.

The Mersey Beat sound helped make Liverpool the most exciting place in the world for teen music fans.

The Cavern may have been packed to its low ceiling most nights, but that didn't cramp the style of the people who danced the night away there.

And it wasn't just The Cavern where it was happening – there were bands in venues like the Iron Door, the Mardi Gras, The Blue Angel and Orrell Park Ballrooms.

Gordon West and Brian Labone present the Liverpool World Cup Queen prize to Miss Sheila Forrest, at The Grafton Ballrooms

The trendiest place in town – the basement of the Everyman in 1967

Working heroes: Enjoying the end of their shift at a Derby Road pub, mid 1960s. Picture courtesy of Tom Patterson

Blame it on the bellboy – Hollywood star Gregory Peck pauses for autographs at The Adelphi Hotel

Do you come here often? Dancing the night away at The Cavern

Rory Storm and the Hurricanes, Central Station, June 1964

Tuning in – The Searchers, fronted by the 'Kirkdale Kid', John McNally

Mersey Beat rocks the world

Time was ripe for a new sound

THE youth of the Sixties wanted something more – and found it in the Mersey Beat sound.

The Sunday night Cavern jazz sessions were soon infiltrated by the first wave of Mersey Beat groups like the Blue Genes before they became the Swinging Blue Jeans.

The first beat night at Number 10 Mathew Street was in May, 1961, and on stage were Rory Storm and the Hurricanes, and Cass and the Cassanovas. From that night The Cavern was given over to rock and roll.

The Mersey venues were what helped the Mersey Beat scene tick, according to Bill Harry, creator of the popular Mersey Beat newspaper in the Sixties.

"To me, the second most important club in Liverpool was the Blue Angel in Seel Street," Bill says. When we were at art college, John Lennon, Stuart Sutcliffe and I used to hang around at the Jacaranda in Slater Street a lot.

"I remember in 1960 when the Beatles first began to play in the tiny cellar there.

"Another coffee bar was the Zodiac in Duke Street where Cilla Black used to serve coffee.

"Regulars included The Hurricanes, with Ringo Starr, and The Big Three.

"Liverpool was a cauldron of talent then and not just Mersey Beat groups. We used to go to Gregson's Well and listen to the Spinners, who always had a packed house at the pub.

"We also used to visit Sampson and Barlows in London Road which at one time was a country music venue, the Black Cat Club, a rock venue, the Cassanova Club and finally the Peppermint Lounge, run by the Blott Brothers who also managed groups such as Earl Royce and the Olympics and the Blackwells. Merseyside was also called the Nashville of the North, and an annual Grand Ole Opry was held at the Philharmonic with outfits such as Hank Walters and the Dusty Road Ramblers, Phil Brady and the Ranchers and the Hillsiders.

"Because there were so many venues for the groups to play in, more than 400 groups were able to develop and thrive in the early 1960s.

"It was the best of times."

The Merseybeats play to a packed Cavern in November 1964

Here come the Brits – John Lennon, Ringo Starr and Paul McCartney, with Cilla Black and Rolling Stone Brian Jones

The Swinging Blue Jeans depart Liverpool Airport for a tour of Sweden, Finland and Denmark, 1965

ADMISSION THURSDAY, 2/6.
13 TEMPLE STREET
(off Victoria and Dale Streets)

TO-NIGHT, Modern Jazz, Ken O'Hara Trio.—Leasowe Tennis Club. Guests 2/-.

MEMBERS PROGRAMME
MARDI GRAS JAZZ CLUB
Mount Pleasant (Near Adelphi Hotel).
TO-NIGHT!
THE SAVOY JAZZMEN!
ALSO
THE MIKE WILSON TRIO
PLUS!
GREAT JAM SESSION!

AT THE CAVERN
Mathew Street (off North John Street)
TO-MORROW (Wednesday):
ROCK NIGHT
with
CASS AND THE CASSANOVAS,
RORY STORM & THE HURRICANES.
ROCK EVERY WEDNESDAY
Admission: (Members) 2/6 before 8 p.m.
AT THE CAVERN
Central 1591.

DANCING

RIALTO LUXURY BALLROOM
ROYAL 4576.
"THE BIG THREE"
For Your Dancing Entertainment.
1. Liverpool's GAYEST BALLROOM.
2. Merseyside's FINEST ORCHESTRA.
3. AND THE FRIENDLIEST ATMOSPHERE IN THE NORTH OF ENGLAND.
TO-MORROW:
MIDWEEK DANCE DATE.

GRAFTON ROOMS.
P.D.C., To-night Area Finals. "Dance News" British Junior/Juvenile Old Time Tales. P.D.C. Novice Veleta Trophy. Dancing 7.30 to 12..

VICTOR SILVESTER STUDIO

CENTRAL CAR H
SERVICES
BOOK YOUR HOLIDAY
NOW
1960 ANGLIAS, PREFECTS,
HILLMANS, DAUPHINES,
VICTORS, FARINA A.40's,
CONVERTIBLES AND
No Deposit.
11/13 Parr St., Liverpool 1.

The birth of Merseybeat – the first all rock 'n' roll bill at The Cavern, May 25, 1960

Stan Kelly gives it some welly at the Bluecoat. Stan Kelly-Bootle, to give him his full name, was the godfather of the Liverpool folk scene

The Fourmost

Making the News **1963**

GERRY'S RECORD BREAKING ROLL

AT the height of Mersey Beat, homegrown talent dominated the hit parade.

In 1963 it was a close run as to who was more popular in Liverpool – Gerry and the Pacemakers or the Beatles. But Gerry in fact set a record that the Beatles could never beat, with his first three singles rocketing straight to Number One. On April 11, How Do You Do It? became the first record by a Liverpool band to top the chart. It was written for Adam Faith and previously had been recorded by the Beatles. The songs I Like It and You'll Never Walk Alone hit the top spot later that same year and history was made.

memorable movies!

NATIONAL HEADLINES

January Britain has the worst winter since 1948. Snow continues until April in some areas.

14 February The Labour Party elects Harold Wilson as its new leader.

5 June John Profumo, Secretary of State for War, resigns over his affair with Christine Keeler.

8 August Thieves ambush the Glasgow to Euston mail train and steal over £2m in used, untraceable banknotes. The biggest ever raid on a British train becomes known as The Great Train Robbery.

18 October Prime Minister Harold Macmillan resigns on the grounds of ill health.

22 November John F Kennedy is assassinated by a gunman in Dallas, Texas, when three shots are fired at his open-topped car.

23 November Lyndon Baines Johnson begins his new job as US president.

24 November Lee Harvey Oswald, the man accused of assassinating John F Kennedy, is shot dead in a Dallas police station. The shooting is captured live on television.

Top of the Pops

Gerry and the Pacemakers – How Do You Do It?
The Beatles – From Me To You
The Searchers – Sweets For My Sweet
Billy J Kramer & The Dakotas – Bad To Me
Brian Poole and the Tremeloes – Do You Love Me

Red carpet rolled out for Beatlemania

We love you, yeah, yeah, yeah!

MERSEYWOOD glamour came to London Road on July 10, 1964, when the Odeon became the setting for the northern premiere of the Beatles' first film, A Hard Day's Night.

It was a Hollywood-style occasion – far superior to the film's earlier Royal premiere in London. It was a big day for both the Beatles and Liverpool and thousands turned out to get a glimpse of the Fab Four.

Afterwards the Beatles were given a civic reception hosted by the city council.

Before it was split into five cinemas, the Odeon in London Road was one enormous picture palace and the 1969 film The Magic Christian, in which Ringo Starr co-starred with Peter Sellers, was also given its premiere there.

Ferry 'Cross The Mersey cashed in on the rising popularity of the Mersey Beat scene in 1965. Starring Gerry Marsden, this foot-tapping pop musical was the first and only film about beat music made in Liverpool during the Mersey boom and featured cameos from Cilla Black and Jimmy Saville.

Of course the biggest hit for Gerry and the Pacemakers was You'll Never Walk Alone, a song which had enthralled Marsden since he saw the film Carousel in his youth.

The 1960s were the decade of change, when bold young people snapped the seals to release the old taboos. Lust, greed, booze and parental neglect were all there in A Taste of Honey (1961) starring Rita Tushingham. It was a wonderful time of challenge and promise for 'Tush' – the grocer's daughter from Hunts Cross, Liverpool – who became one of the most famous faces in the country.

Left: Crowds follow the Beatles' cars, as they head up Dale Street from the Town Hall to the Odeon, for the premiere of A Hard Day's Night

Right: Rita Tushingham in A Taste Of Honey

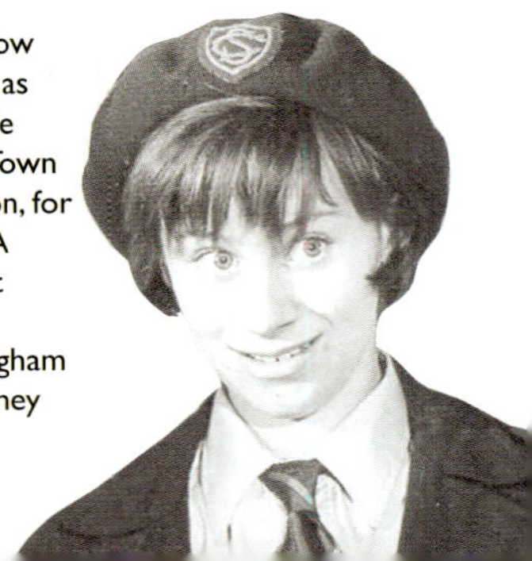

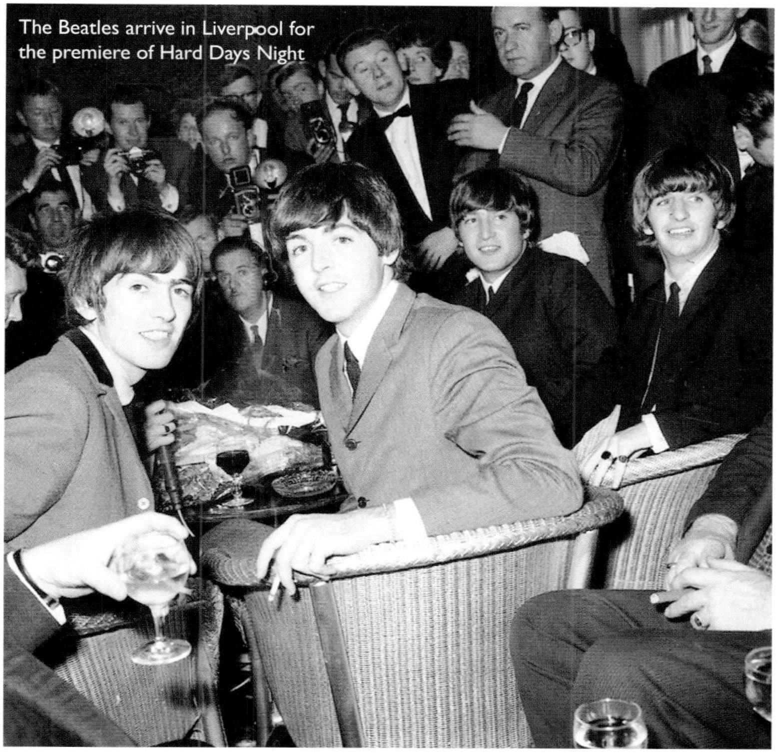

The Beatles arrive in Liverpool for the premiere of Hard Days Night

Tom Bell and Olivia Hussey, filming All The Right Noises in Liverpool, June 1969

There were three cinemas on Lime Street, the Futurist, Liverpool's first purpose- built cinema, The Plaza, and the Forum

Gerry 'Cross the Mersey: On George's Landing Stage before filming

Striking out on television

A flame burns and flickers

Filming at the docks for The Big Flame; Ken Jones as Freddie and Tom West as a policeman

THE '60s was the golden age of television and Liverpool was a major player in shaping what we now all watch today.

Writers and performers honed their craft in that mould-breaking, creative decade when new and radical ideas were encouraged. Scouse Proud The Army Game (1957 - 61), starring Norman Rossington, a Scouse stalwart of stage and screen, was the first time a Scouse accent had been heard across the nation via the telly.

One show that had its comic clangers was Z-Cars. Lots of viewers treasure the memory of those giveaway sequences that had Fancy Smith in a pub brawl one minute and still breathing heaving and looking dishevelled in the next scene which was supposed to be taking place the next morning.

But Liverpool always provided a gritty backdrop for no nonsense dramas on stage, TV and film.

In 1969 one TV play showed the nation the earthy, rebellious Liverpool spirit.

It focused on a prolonged industrial dispute at Liverpool Docks, the striking workers rejected management demands of a return to work and decided instead to occupy the docks and run the operation themselves.

'The Big Flame' was writer Jim Allen's second work for the inspirational Wednesday Play series. It was his first with director Kenneth Loach. Producer was the well-respected Tony Garnett.

The 85 minute black and white play was filmed in Loach's much-copied drama-documentary style and on the windy locations of Liverpool's Albert Dock.

In the Big Flame real dockers appeared alongside up and coming actors. Ken Jones would become a major TV star and Peter Kerrigan would be a name to look out for.

It was on 16mm film, giving the picture the same quality as newsreel footage.

Mary Whitehouse, secretary of the National Viewers' and Listeners' Association, complained that the play was "a blueprint for the communist takeover of the docks" and wrote to both Prime Minister Harold Wilson and Conservative leader Ted Heath to urge a review of the BBC's charter.

Loach returned to the subject of industrial disputes on the Liverpool docks for his 1997 film The Flickering Flame.

Tony Booth with Warren Mitchell, off to watch his beloved West Ham

Private 'Cupcake' Cook: Norman Rossington

Z-Cars

Philip King's farce I'll Get My Man, at the Royal Court. Pictured left to right, Peter Barkworth with Liverpool's Tony Booth and Avril Angers

Cilla and Bobby's wedding in 1969

Lorra lorra love for Cilla

A true Liver Bird

ONE of Liverpool's best known former residents was a young music fan called Priscilla White.

The Scotland Road-born star was brought up alongside her three brothers in a two-up two-down above George Murray's Barbers, by her father, a docker and her mother, who ran a stall on a Liverpool market.

She attended St Anthony's before leaving at the age of 14 to begin a typing course at Anfield Commercial College.

By the age of 20, she had progressed from student to full time dictaphone typist, but Cilla Black had greater ambitions. She shot to stardom in 1963 under the management of Brian Epstein and her first two singles, Anyone Who Had a Heart and You're My World, went to number one in the charts.

Over the next two years she had another seven records in the top ten. Bobby Willis, her manager and later her husband, nurtured and encouraged her into Britain's most successful woman entertainer ever.

In 1964 she gave more than 400 performances at the London Palladium. She went on to host Blind Date, which was watched by 17m viewers at the height of its 1980s popularity, for 18 years.

Cilla still is a true star.

Cilla, Billy J Kramer and Gerry Marsden

Right: Even Jimmy Tarbuck himself, became a bendy doll with a Beatle haircut in 1965

Below: Gordon Milne and Peter Thompson admire Tarby's table football style shooting

It's Tarbuck!

The nation's favourite comedian

THE Sixties were a golden decade for Jimmy Tarbuck.

Tarby shot to overnight fame on October 27, 1963, when he appeared on Sunday Night at the London Palladium after being spotted by Val Parnell.

National newspapers raved about his performance and he was on his way to being one of the country's favourite comics. Soon he was appearing with Frankie Vaughan in panto at the Liverpool Empire.

The son of a well-known bookmaker, he was a milkman, car mechanic (sacked for fooling around) and salesman (sacked for telling jokes) before becoming an apprentice hairdresser. His first public appearance was in a talent contest at Butlins and he went on to be a Red Coat.

Since his debut on a programme called Comedy Bandbox, Tarby's had more TV shows bearing his name than almost any other entertainer.

Arise, Sir Doddy

Flying the funny flag over Mirthyside...

NOW that's what you call entertainment, high on a roof with a Liverpool backdrop the dancing girls are out.

But who is that with his head in the clouds?

His hair fluttering in the wind and a smile wider than the Mersey Tunnel.

Black puddings, rampant tickling sticks and a jam butty flying over the Royal Court – what could it mean back in February 1965?

Yes, Missus, by jove, Ken Dodd was in town and up to his record-breaking antics.

Star of stage, Screen, TV, radio and the recording studio, Doddy was – and still is – an ambassador for Liverpool and a place he's always called 'Mirthyside.'

Ken accepted a special 'Doddy' flag to mark his residence at the city's Royal Court theatre – one of his own favourite venues – to celebrate another plumptious milestone in his multi-layered career.

Breaking box office records came naturally to Kenneth Arthur Dodd.

It was estimated that Doddy had been seen by a total audience of more than 250,000. A year earlier he'd done the same.

Doddy, theatre bosses and audiences were tickled that the show was extended three weeks even before it opened.

Months later Doddy was in capital form – wowing them all over again at the London Palladium.

Cardinal John Heenan surrounded by people eager to meet him informerly at St George's Hall in 1967. When he become Archbishop of Westminster in 1963, 125,000 people besieged Lime Street station to see him off

Below: Prime Minister Harold Wilson presents the Challenge Cup to Rugby League legend Alex Murphy, captain of the 1966 St Helens side. The MP for Huyton was an adopted Merseysider – even if he never managed to lose his Yorkshire accent

Liverpool sculptor Arthur Dooley protests outside Bluecoat Chambers in 1968

Some of the artists who appeared at the Everyman for a performance of Lovenight No. 2 in June, 1967 – Graham Layden, Andy Tobarts, Felicity Wren, Roger McGough, Brian Patten, Adrian Henri, Michael McGear, Susanna Crouch, John Gorman

Sound as a pound

Poetry in motion

THE Mersey Beat was dominating the world with its musical onslaught.

But Liverpool was also changing the face of the poetry across the universe.

Bohemian Liverpudlians had always enjoyed getting up and doing a 'turn' in pubs and clubs – but there was also a strong tradition of poets who performed in the cellars, bars and arts venues.

They gained national and international acclaim in the '60s by helping with the rebirth of poetry.

Three men helped shape poetry forever: Roger McGough, Brian Patten and Adrian Henri, all Merseysiders through and through, who collectively became The Mersey Poets with a fresh lively humour and melancholy collection of poems.

In 1967 Penguin published The Mersey Sound which brought the trio's work to wider critical acclaim. Their creative input also involved paintings from Henri and 'happenings in music and performance'.

The individual Mersey Poets pursued solo careers while still retaining their group status. Performance poetry enjoyed a whole new following. The Mersey Sound also did the seemingly impossible – it made it cool to read poetry in school.

The book itself became the biggest selling poetry anthology of all time and would lead to the Mersey Poets one day becoming Freemen of the city of Liverpool.

Roger McGough also joined pop group Scaffold with poets/musicians Mike McCartney and John Gorman.

Making the News
1964

THE BOAT THAT ROCKED

RADIO Caroline rocked the airwaves in 1964, broadcasting the heady excitement of bands like the Beatles and the Rolling Stones, at a time when BBC radio played less than 45 minutes of music every day.

In July '64, MV Caroline, the larger, heavier and stronger vessel of the Caroline 'pirate' fleet, sailed to the Irish Sea and anchored 3.5 miles off the coast of Ramsey, Isle of Man, to become Radio Caroline North. Keeping outside territorial waters, DJs Jerry Leighton, Tom Lodge and Alan Turner made friends with a whole new area of fans, who could now listen to non-stop Sixties hits in all their glory.

The station's supporters soared and not just among youngsters. In 1966, when 140 people were killed after a coalmine slag collapsed on a school in Aberfan, Wales, Labour MP Bessie Braddock launched an appeal in her name over Caroline. As a result, she was able to present a cheque for £8,100 to the Secretary of State for Wales.

In August 1967, the Marine Broadcasting Act came into action and both Caroline North and South became Radio Caroline International. DJs from the North station held a farewell party in the studio, berthed off the Isle of Man. The freewheeling sound of Radio Caroline North was never matched.

memorable movies!

NATIONAL HEADLINES

6 February The British and French governments agree a deal for the construction of the Channel Tunnel.

25 February Cassius Clay is crowned heavyweight champion of the world after beating Sonny Liston.

20 April BBC Two is launched.

12 June Nelson Mandela, The leader of the anti-apartheid struggle in South Africa, is jailed for life for sabotage.

2 July President Lyndon B Johnson signs the Civil Rights Bill.

14 October Mary Rand leaps into sporting history at the Tokyo Olympics with a long jump record of 22 feet 2 inches, earning the first gold medal for Britain in women's athletics.

9 November The House of Commons vote to abolish the death penalty for murder in Britain.

31 December Donald Campbell breaks the world water speed record on Lake Dumbleyung, Perth, Australia.

Top of the Pops

Dave Clark Five – Glad All Over
Cilla Black – Anyone Who Had A Heart
Herman's Hermits (right) – I'm Into Something Good
Sandie Shaw – Always Something There To Remind Me
Roy Orbison (left) – Oh Pretty Woman

From the slipper to the cane

The law of the playground

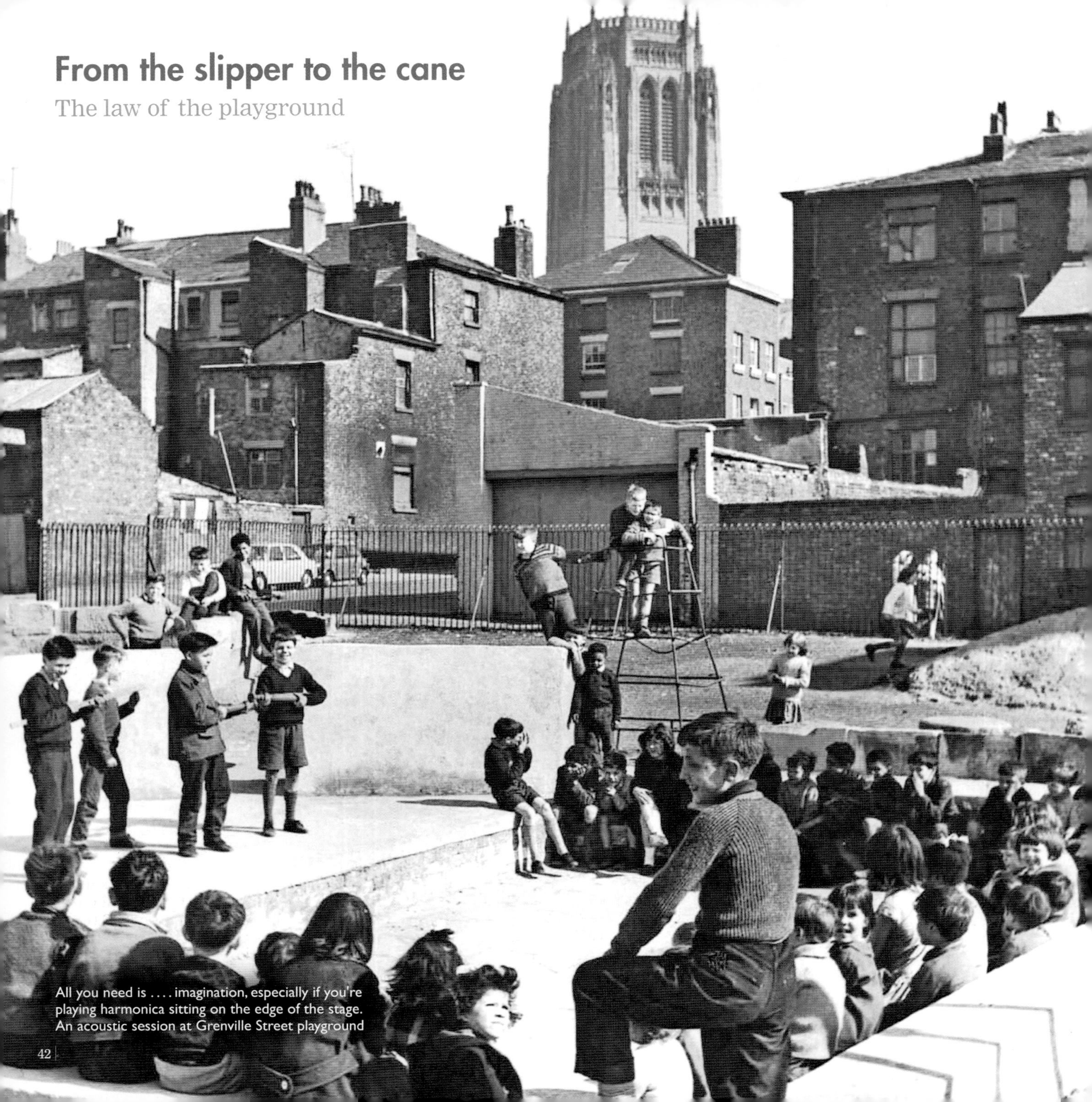

All you need is . . . . imagination, especially if you're playing harmonica sitting on the edge of the stage. An acoustic session at Grenville Street playground

Left: Back to school with a leap for these boys from Holt Comprehensive School, March 1969

Below: While mum shops in Lewis's, these two cheeky monkeys get to meet some of the animals

SIXTIES school life saw the intense learning of the 'Three Rs' – without the aid of computers but there was always an abacus.

No overhead projectors – just blackboard, chalk and duster. And there were plenty of spelling tests. Punishment was eased upon unsuspecting pupils – a real education from the quaint tap of a slipper as infants, to all out hostility in the secondary and grammar regime with the dreaded cane accompanied by the phrase 'six of the best.'

If school dinners weren't bad enough, there was always the intimidating presence of school bullies (always will be) but certainly no drugs or gun crime then.

It was a time of studying for 'O' and 'A' levels and homework was done to a backdrop of Batman on the telly while you munched on a Wagon Wheel.

In the playground girls skipped on ropes or danced in hoops while budding Bobby Moores were inspired by the England World Cup success and swapped soccer cards with a real passion…a Pele for a Roger Hunt or Alan Ball.

We had free milk until 1968 when it was abolished in secondary schools.

In the next decade a certain politician called Thatcher would stop free school milk for children over the age of seven.

The travelling dentists and doctors called in and the 'nit nurse' had her work cut out with the lads since lice was difficult to find in the army of many long-haired pupils.

Those who were learned University or Polytechnic status could enjoy a student grant of £12 a term. Meanwhile the revolutionary Open University gave us home study with a difference in 1969.

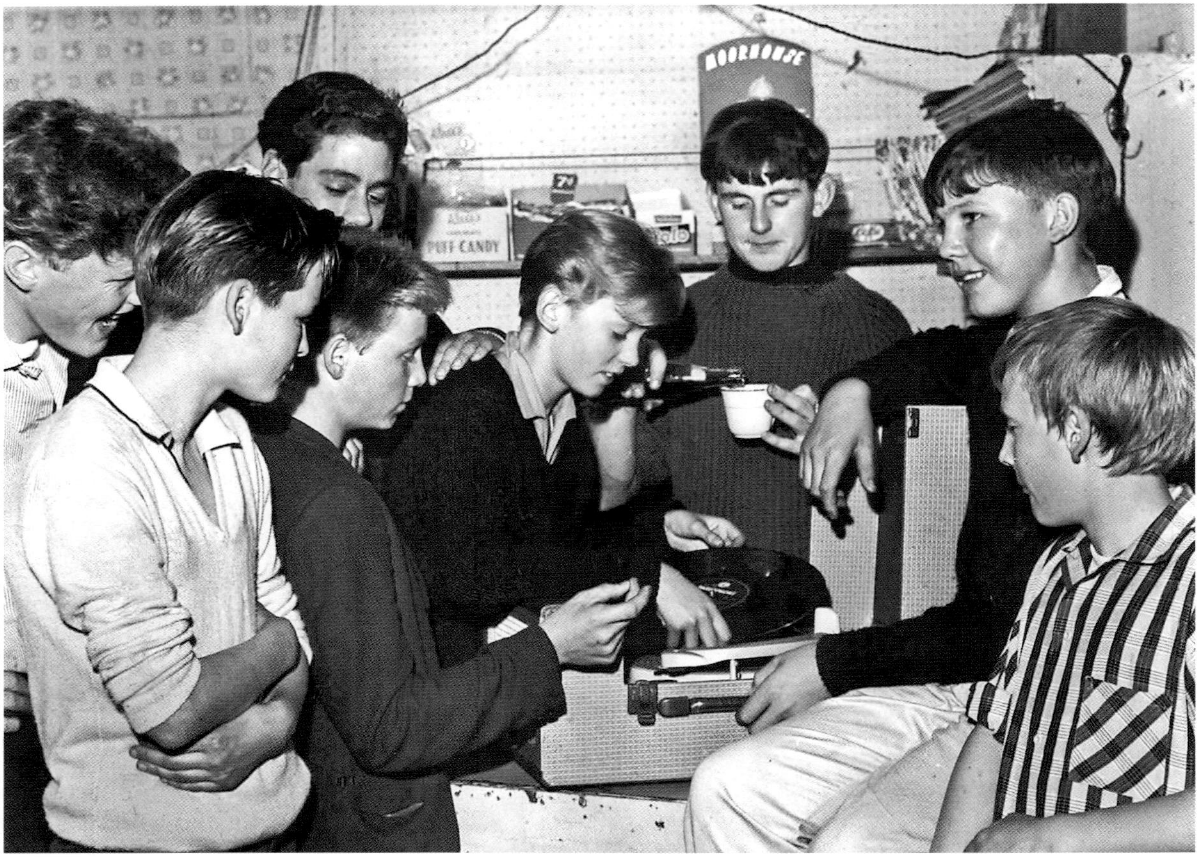

Top: A lively record session around Heswall Boy's Club's canteen counter, 24 August 1964

Left: Youngsters at the 17th International Summer Camp at Colomendy, July 1968

Far left: Life was just one big adventure in the summer of 1966

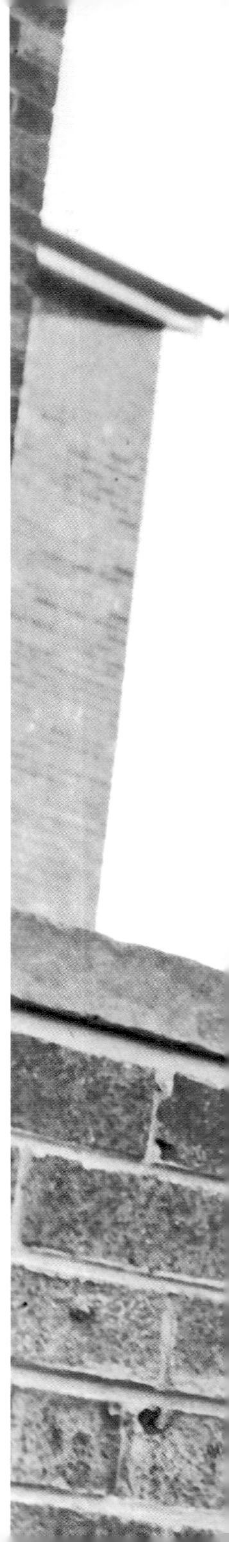

Our gang...

"'Mind yer car Mister?"

A splashing time during floods at Aintree

A finger flicking good game

BLOW football was a real inspiration when it arrived on the toy scene allowing two players with two straws, a light ball, a couple of tiny goalies and two goals.

Blow me – that was inspired. It was, as the box said,'footy fun for all the family' even if you couldn't keep up the breath level for 90 minutes. Footy fans could create their own Match of The Day, everyday. But progress of the high-tech variety would change all that. When real footy seasons ended in the sixties there was one way of keeping the soccer frenzy momentum going during the summer lay off – home and away – with Subbuteo.

The board game really took the country's imagination especially after the 1966 World Cup.

This indoor table sport was tweaked and honed in the early '60s and became a real passion for those who wanted to keep their own club's flag flying. Intricate strip designs could make you your very own manager and extra accessories helped make the games even more realistic with floodlights, press crews.

Everton V Liverpool derbies were just as heated. Mini-leagues sprouted up in living rooms across Liverpool. All you needed was the ability dexterity and skill to flick your tiny player on his own semi circular base in the right direction.

Successful platers would compete for mini silver FA cup replicas. You could even bring along your own supporters too mum and dad,school mates.

Subbuteo was simply finger-flicking good. But if you wanted to be a bit more macho there was always Action Man soldier dolls to score with from a sailor to a pilot – based on the American GI Joe model.

You could create your own war hero and dress him up in all the latest military attire and gadgets.

Action Man even attracted the romantic types enjoying flings with Sindy Dolls who were becoming fashion icons in their own right. Chewits and Taveners wine gums were the sweets for my sweet – unless you were George Harrison, who got bombarded by Jelly Babies on stage after admitting he loved their wibbly-wobbly world.

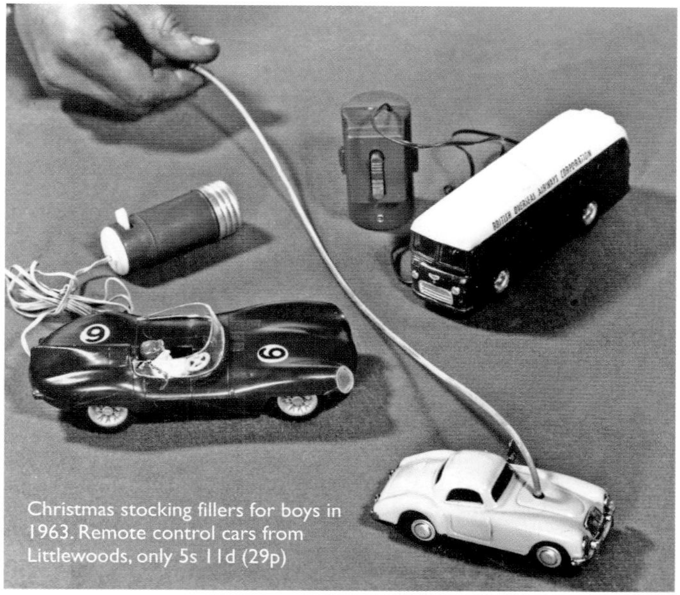

Christmas stocking fillers for boys in 1963. Remote control cars from Littlewoods, only 5s 11d (29p)

Above: A Saturday morning mecca for thousands of boys, Hobbies in Basnett Street – everything from Meccano and Hornby to air pistols and Airfix

Right: Learning road safety with toys at Wallasey's first Tufty Club in 1962

Stink bombs, fake poo, itching powder and exploding cigarettes. The Wizards Den in Moorfields, Liverpool's home of fun

Making the News

1965

THE VILLAGE THAT DROWNED

THE controversial flooding of the small rural Welsh village of Capel Celyn to create a reservoir to supply Liverpool's expected population growth is now recognised as one of the most momentous and tragic episodes in Welsh – and arguably English – political history of the 20th century.

When the plan was first announced, Liverpool pleaded that it needed the extra water to cope with expected industrial growth and its city centre slum clearance programme. The Corporation intoned rather pompously: "The people of Liverpool are becoming more sanitary."

The plan drawn up by Liverpool Corporation was passed as the Tryweryn Bill on August 1, 1957. Thousands marched in opposition to the scheme, 35 out of 36 Welsh MPs voted against it and protests continued right up to the official opening of Llyn Celyn in October 1965, when Liverpool Corporation organised a 'celebration' party. But all protests were ignored and the village of Capel Celyn was lost forever.

In 2005, Liverpool City Council officially apologised for what had happened.

"We realise the hurt of forty years ago when the Tryweryn Valley was transformed into a reservoir to help meet the water needs of Liverpool," said Mike Storey. "For any insensitivity by our predecessor council at that time, we apologise and hope that the historic and sound relationship between Liverpool and Wales can be completely restored."

memorable movies!

NATIONAL HEADLINES

7 January Identical twin brothers Ronnie and Reggie Kray are arrested on suspicion of running a protection racket in London.

30 January Thousands attend Winston Churchill's funeral, who died after suffering a stroke on 24 January. He was 90-years-old.

18 June The British government announces plans for the introduction of a blood alcohol limit for drivers in its clampdown on drink-driving.

27 July Edward Heath becomes leader of the Conservative Party.

29 July The Beatles' film Help! debuts in London.

1 August Cigarette advertising is banned from television.

29 October Ian Brady and Myra Hindley appear in court, charged with the murders of Edward Evans (17), Lesley Ann Downey (10) and John Kilbride (12).

22 December A 70 mph speed limit is imposed on British roads.

Top of the Pops

Seekers – The Carnival Is Over
Sonny & Cher (left) – I Got You Babe
Ken Dodd – Tears
The Byrds – Mr Tambourine Man
The Beatles – Day Tripper / We Can Work It Out

You didn't have to be old, male and bald to be a member, but it certainly helped – the floor of the Liverpool Stock Exchange in 1962

Knuckling down to a 'proper job'

Or how to add another string to your guitar

IT was Paul McCartney who said he became a Beatle because he 'didn't want to have a proper job.'

If his singing didn't work out in the '60s he could have pursued a career in Lewis's department store where he worked as a teenager or he could have followed his dad in the Cotton Exchange.

George Harrison could have been an electrician in Blacklers or driven a Corpy (corporation) bus like his dad. Richard Starkey had dreams of being a hairdresser.

A young John Lennon wanted to be an artist – anything but a merchant seaman like his dad and so many other Liverpudlian men.

Many workers disillusioned with their own jobs would quit during the fluctuating '60s job market in the knowledge that there were institutions such as The Labour Exchange to make it easier to move from one job to another.

Liverpool had its fair share of big name companies with matching workforces. The Mersey Docks, Tate and Lyle's, Ford and Littlewoods, were just a few household names where generations had worked all their lives.

The '60s was a time when apprenticeships, too, were in abundance.

For the adventurous, the Army, RAF and Navy had flourishing recruiting offices in the city.

Liverpool's football talent prayed that a scout would spot them leading to a great escape to the fields of Goodison or Anfield.

Aspiring entertainers worked the factories and offices by day and the clubs by night.

The '60s were a time when you could actually meet a real life ' School Career's Advisor' . . . but it was up to you whether you took their advice or not. Many didn't.

Ladies hard at work at the English Electric Companys fusegear department, on the East Lancs Road

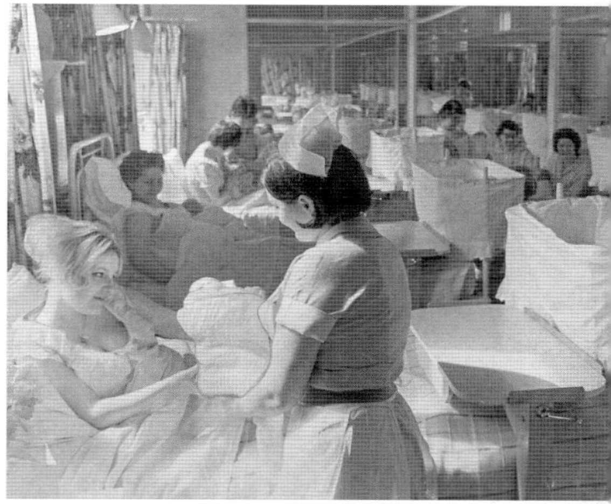

Walton Hospital Maternity Unit, 1968

Above: Policewomen Joan Jackson and Ruth Phillips on patrol, February 1964

Left: Liverpool Police get mobile in 1967 with their fleet of Mini Cooper S's, Ford Anglias and Triumph 650s

The coastal minesweeper HMS Mersey, seen at Seacombe landing stage 1960

River of dreams

But the push for change is not all plain sailing

THE port of Liverpool built its reputation as the gateway to the western world.

In the Sixties, the throbbing port was Liverpool's greatest industry. Stretching from the Gladstone in the north to the Herculaneum in the south, the port had a seven-mile long line of docks and basins with 27 miles of quays.

And across the river, there were the Birkenhead docks with more than nine miles of quay. Installations varied from the gigantic accommodation for the big Atlantic liners down to the smallest coaster.

But strikes by dockers were common in the Sixties as the men fought to protect their jobs in a changing world. In 1967 a strike broke out that lasted six weeks and paralysed the port of Liverpool from September 18 to October 30. Thousands of dockers, sometimes up to 8,000 men, met at the Pier Head to hold meetings during the strike.

They voted repeatedly to remain on strike until their demands for parity with London rates and conditions were met. The Liverpool Echo reported at the time that 9,785 dockers were on strike and 11 ships idle. Harold Wilson flew to Liverpool to see if he could bring an end to the dispute.

It finally ended when more than 6,000 men meeting at the Pier Head decided to go back to work.

In the Sixties the Mersey Docks and Harbour Board made a £1m conversion of the Gladstone Graving Dock into a deep-water berth, pending the £32m port extension scheme at Seaforth.

At times people could still see the stacks of the liners above the Landing Stage buildings; the Empresses of the Canadian Pacific, Elder Dempter's Apapa and Aurial, that went on the West African run, and the occasional children's cruise ship. There was still work for those on the Stage, but the big ships, like the Mauretania, Scythia and Samaria of the Cunard Line, berthed no more in Liverpool. It marked the end of a glorious era.

In the Sixties, the throbbing port was still Liverpool's greatest industry

A Vauxhall Viva heading for Canada in 1965, where it was the best selling imported car in that year

The tug strike ends as a flotilla heads out of Calderstone Dock, Bootle for work

Crowds gather on Princes Landing Stage to greet the Empress of Canada, before her passengers board for voyage to Montreal, April 24 1961

Cunard Liners' RMS Carinthia from New York, Feb 6, 1960

A mammoth crane loads equipment at Gladstone Dock, bound for a Hungarian ammonia factory

The Cunard liner Caronia moves slowly away from Gladstone Dock after her annual overhaul

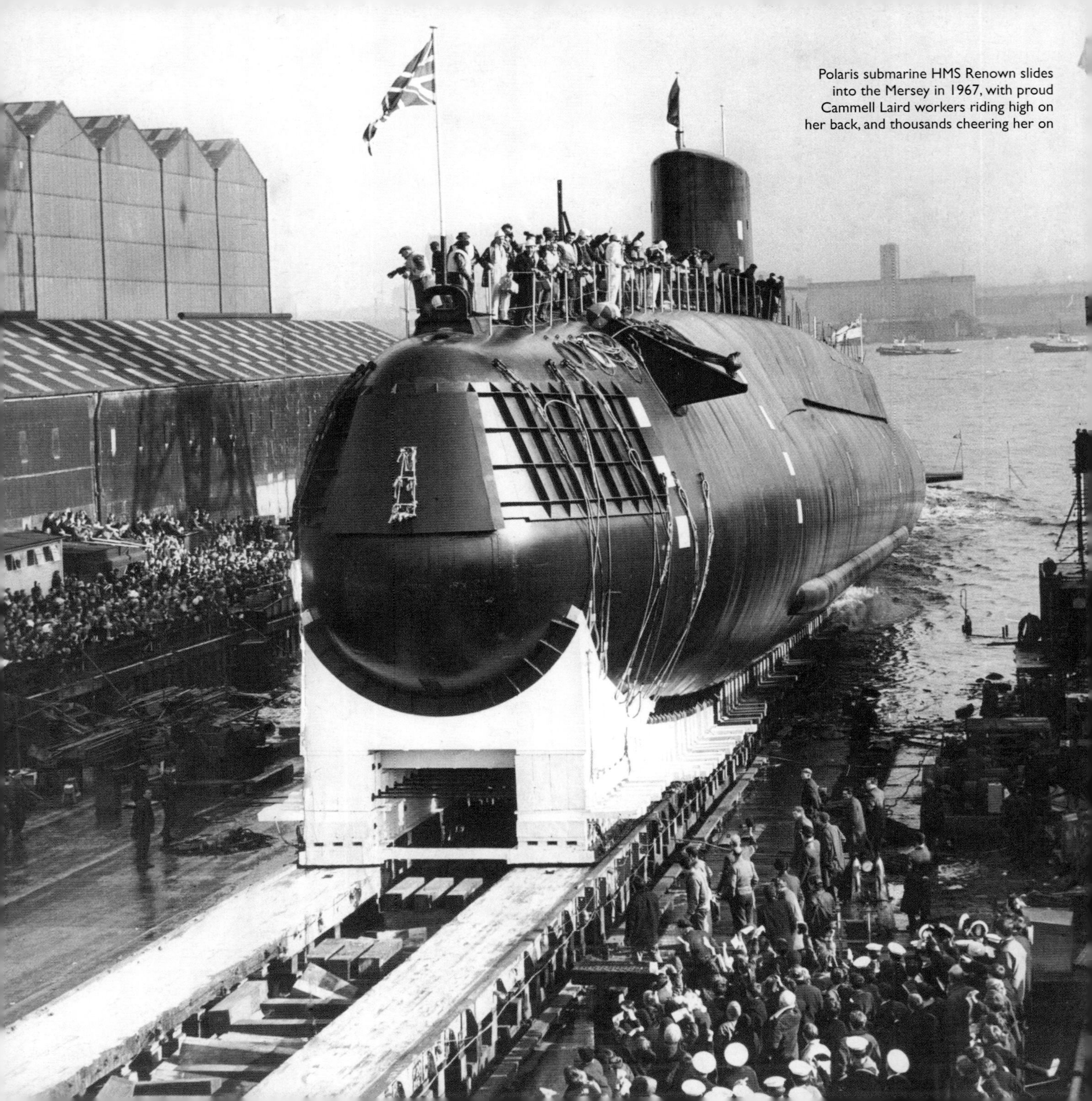

Polaris submarine HMS Renown slides into the Mersey in 1967, with proud Cammell Laird workers riding high on her back, and thousands cheering her on

Making the News

1966

WORLD CUP COMES TO GOODISON

EVERTONIANS will assure you that quality players turning out at Goodison Park is a fortnightly occurance, but even the most die-hard Blue must concede that the famous stadium has witnessed nothing like the glittering array of stars on parade in the 1966 World Cup.

Goodison was chosen as one of the grounds for the tournament and four of the five matches staged there thrilled the public, producing some great goals.

Pele, Garrincha, Jairzinho, Gerson and Tostao from Brazil; Beckenbauer, Seeler and Overath from West Germany; Eusebio and Torres from Portugal; Bene and Albert from Hungary, plus legendary Russian keeper Yashin, were all on view, displaying breathtaking moments of their undoubted talent.

Pele of Brazil trudges off as his side lose to Portugal 3-1 during the World Cup

Eusebio of Portugal

memorable movies!

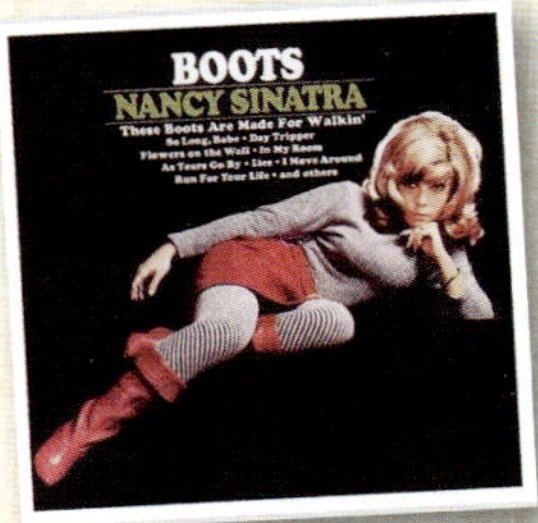

NATIONAL HEADLINES

3 February The Russian probe Luna 9 makes the first controlled landing of a spacecraft on the Moon.

4 March In an interview published in The Evening Standard, John Lennon comments "We're more popular than Jesus now."

31 March The Labour Party under Harold Wilson win the general election.

2 June Moors murderers Ian Brady and Myra Hindley sentenced to life imprisonment for three child murders committed between 1963 and 1965.

29 June The United States lands its first spacecraft on the Moon.

30 July Barclays Bank introduces the first British credit card.

30 July England beat West Germany 4-2 to win the World Cup at Wembley.

21 October 144 people, 116 of them children, are killed by a coal slag heap tipping at Aberfan, near Merthyr Tydfil in Wales.

1 November Viet Cong artillery shell the South Vietnamese capital, Saigon. US President General Dwight D Eisenhower called for more troops to be sent to Vietnam to bring about a swift end to the conflict.

Top of the Pops

Four Tops – Reach Out I'll Be There
Jim Reeves – Distant Drums
The Kinks – Sunny Afternoon
Nancy Sinatra – These Boots Are Made For Walkin'
Tom Jones – Green, Green Grass Of Home

Grand symbols of the city

Shirts, suits, ties, hats, underwear and shoes – going up

DURING the early 1960s, the Lewis's store became part of the Beatles' legend by first employing a young Paul McCartney as a temp, and then becoming the regular meeting place for John Lennon and his girlfriend, and later, wife, Cynthia.

The statue itself was immortalised in the song, In My Liverpool Home, with the line "We meet under a statue exceedingly bare".

Liverpool had more than its fair share of great department stores and each and every one played a major part in the experience of shopping in the city – Owen Owen, TJs or Ethel Austin, the brand for thrifty young mothers.

You could drive past George Henry Lee's to a true city centre that had not yet been turned into a bus rank. Bon Marche with its French fashions, perfumes and accessories was renowned for being at the height of fashion and of the highest standard. In 1961 Bon Marche was merged with George Henry Lee and joined by a covered walkway. Blacklers was a grand symbol of the city, filling six floors – and who could forget Blackie the rocking horse near the men's department? At Christmas time people queued as far as the eye could see to visit Father Christmas and the fabulous grotto that was there every year.

According to one Liverpool shop manager interviewed at the time, people started to gather their gifts a lot later: "The Christmas shopping season once lasted four or five weeks.

"Nowadays people leave their shopping to the last 10 or 12 days – it's the new modern trend!"

You went to St John's Market for a bargain and you got one. Shopping was a cosy affair. There was no queuing at checkouts, the ringing of the old fashioned till was still to be heard.

Side by side with the street newspaper sellers were the barrow boys and flower girls. Most famous among them, selling daffs outside Central Station in all weathers, was Lizzie Christian.

Lane-control outside Blacklers, Great Charlotte Street

Christmas shopping in Lewis's, December 3, 1966

5 11

The Wholesale Fish Market,
Great Charlotte Street, Liverpool

Pre-pedestrian age
Church Street

Woolies on Stanley Road, Bootle, with some
other fine shopping names including
Johnsons, Burton's distinctive art deco facade
and Peter Pell, back in October, 1961

The Costa living – shoppers at the travel bureau in Lewis's

The old St John's Market

Christmas shoppers pack the narrow pavements on Church Street in 1966

Electric dreams

Diamonds in the drudgery

IN the home, labour-saving devices were taking some of the drudgery out of housework in the Sixties.

A Liverpool shop in 1960 was selling Hotpoint washing machines at £67 but people could spread the cost by putting down 44 shillings deposit and paying 9s 6d a week.

Vacuum cleaners were selling from around £10 at the start of the decade.

Music was popular and you could get a radiogram, with "hi-fi stylus and twin speakers" for £40.

You could pick up a new three-piece suite for 54gns and wardrobes for 13 gns. But wages then could be from as little as £6 a week.

Hard coke and coal was used to keep the home fires burning but oil-fired central heating was gradually being introduced to homes throughout Liverpool and the rest of the country.

The oil revolution came about when the smelly black-enamelled paraffin stove gave way to the sleek, streamlined convector. From then on coal was doomed. Fridges were advertised in the Liverpool Echo from around £39 upwards. We went to work on an egg, bread was white and almost every home had a chip pan.

Housewives were still expected to sew and do traditional jobs in the home and were often treated in a patronising way that their sisters in the future would not have tolerated.

China Street may be due for demolition but there's still time to donkey stone the front step while chatting with the neighbours in 1965

Open all hours: Counter culture before the age of the supermarket

Where's the 'on' switch?

Making the News
1967

WELCOME TO THE 'WIGWAM'

THE opening of Liverpool's Roman Catholic Metropolitan Cathedral in 1967 marked an important milestone in the history of the city as well as the Church.

In 1960, the Archbishop of Liverpool, John Carmel Heenan, announced an architectural competition to produce a completely new building to seat 2,000, which would relate to the existing Crypt and be capable of construction within five years.

Of 300 entries from all over the world, Sir Frederick Gibberd's design was chosen and building began in October 1962.

It was completed less than five years later, on May 13 1967. Affectionately nicknamed Paddy's Wigwam, the Cathedral was consecrated in the presence of the Papal Legate, Cardinal Heenan, the Duke of Norfolk representing the Queen, the Prime Minister Harold Wilson and Mr Edward Heath, Leader of the Opposition.

Thousands attended the event and Paddy's Wigwam became as vital a part of the Liverpool skyline along with the huge Liverpool Cathedral at the other end of Hope Street, and the Pier Head.

memorable movies!

NATIONAL HEADLINES

31 March At London Astoria, Jimi Hendrix sets fire to his guitar on stage for the first time.

8 April Sandi Shaw wins the Eurovision Song Contest for the United Kingdom with Puppet On A String.

14 July The Roman Catholic Liverpool Metropolitan Cathedral is consecrated.

1 July BBC2 broadcast its first colour pictures from Wimbledon.

27 August Brian Epstein is found dead in his Belgravia home in London. The death is officially ruled as an accidental overdose of sleeping pills.

30 September BBC Radio One is launched.

16 October Rallies across America take place in 30 US cities, to protest against the continuing war in Vietnam.

18 December A ban on the movement of farm animals is imposed across the whole of England and Wales in an attempt to curb the spread of the foot-and-mouth epidemic.

11 December Supersonic aircraft Concorde is unveiled in France.

Top of the Pops

The Monkees – I'm A Believer
Engelbert Humperdinck – Release Me
Scott McKenzie – San Francisco
Procul Harem (left) – A Whiter Shade of Pale
The Beatles – Hello Goodbye

Blue heaven: Brian Labone holds the FA Cup aloft at the 1966 final against Sheffield Wednesday. Overshadowed in the middle is double goal-scorer Mike Trebilcock

Champions of the world

Wingless wonders soar to new heights

RIGHT through from club to international level, English teams emerged as competitors to be feared and respected in the Sixties.

The icing on the cake was when England won the World Cup in 1966 with Sir Alf Ramsey's 'wingless wonders'. It was his idea for full backs to become wingers, when necessary, and wingers to drop back and be defenders. English soccer was evolving.

This exciting development was being spearheaded by our two great clubs, Everton and Liverpool. The men behind the Anfield and Goodison masterplans were two of the greatest ever managers seen in Liverpool – Bill Shankly and Harry Catterick.

The 46-year-old Shankly was appointed Liverpool manager in December, 1959, with an annual salary of £2,500, and went on to create a legend. He rebuilt the team with new signings Ian St John and Ron Yeats, bargain buys from his native Scotland, and Liverpool ended the 1961-62 season as champions. Only two years after winning the Second Division title, Liverpool were League Champions with virtually the same players that had won them promotion.

They won the title again in 1965-66 and 1966-67 and the FA Cup in 1964-65.

Harry Catterick was plucked from the obscurity of Cheadle Heath Nomads and as a bustling centre forward, notched 24 goals in 71 post-war games with Everton before moving to Crewe Alexandra.

After management experience with Rochdale and Sheffield Wednesday he accepted the Everton hot seat in 1961. He enjoyed tremendous success and his achievements compared with the likes of Shankly, Busby and Revie. Under his management, the Blues finished outside the top six on only one occasion and that was in 1966 when they won the FA Cup.

They won the First Division championship in 1962-63 and 1969-70, and were FA Cup runners-up in 1968.

Renowned as a strict disciplinarian, Catterick inherited a galaxy of stars and turned them into First Division champions within two years. Catterick confirmed money could buy success and he wheeled and dealed in the transfer market to strengthen his playing staff.

After his plans were disrupted when Tony Kay was jailed in the football bribes trial in 1965, Catterick concentrated on grooming homegrown talents and produced one of the most entertaining football teams of all time.

We are the greatest – Everton fans watch Cassius Clay ahead of his fight with Henry Cooper, on the day of the FA Cup final against Sheffield Wednesday

World class – Gerry Byrne, Ian Callaghan and Roger Hunt are presented with tankards from the Lord mayor of Liverpool, in recognition of their selection for England's 1966 Squad

Clash of the Titans.
Two great captains, Roy Vernon and Ron Yeats, shake hands before the September 1962 derby at Goodison

The Red Army – Liverpool supporters board the train at Lime Street, on their way to the 1965 FA Cup Final against Leeds United

Peter Thomson shows off his trophy after winning the 1965 Open Golf Championship at Royal Birkdale

A challenge for swing and mind: Arnold Palmer, at Birkdale in 1961, did much to promote the Open

National legends: It was a chance ride for former Olympic showjumper Eddie Harty on Highland Wedding in 1969, after regular pilot Owen McNally broke his elbow in the build-up to the big race

Left: 100-1 outsider Foinavon was the beneficiary of mayhem caused at the 23rd fence by a riderless horse in 1967. The fence now bears the name of this remarkable winner

Right: Looking amazingly composed after thirty gruelling jumps, Red Alligator (with Brian Fletcher in the saddle) comes over the last fence to win the 1968 Grand National in convincing style

Johnny Cooke retained the British Welterweight title against Shaun Doyle at the Liverpool Stadium in 1967

Hero of the underdog

Cooke sets Stadium alight

DESPITE boxing struggling to attract sell-out crowds at the Liverpool Stadium, there were some fine boxers associated with the venue, with Johnny Cooke one of the stand-out boxers during the decade.

Cooke had enjoyed an impressive amateur career, losing only 26 of his 368 contests. He finally turned professional in 1960, but at the age of 25 many people thought he had left it too late. Over the course of the next 11 years, during which he had 93 contests, Cooke was to prove the sceptics wrong.

Upon turning professional, Cooke, unlike some of his contemporaries who went looking for big paydays down south, chose to remain on Merseyside.

Despite taking four years to get a British welterweight title opportunity, he would win the belt at the second time of asking, winning an all-Liverpool affair against the undefeated Brian McCaffrey in February 1967.

Cooke fought for the European welterweight title, while also successfully defending his British title against Shaun Doyle of Barnsley, and securing the vacant British Empire title by defeating Lennox Beckles. Both contests took place at the Stadium, and would prove highpoints of his career.

Cooke should be remembered as one of Merseyside's finest champions, a man that proved many of the sceptics wrong.

Making the News 1968

END OF THE LINE FOR STEAM

BARELY a moment after a whooshing noise from the engine filled the air, the railway station platform became lost in a mist of white smoke.

Children laughed, cameras clicked and slowly the gleaming steam engine began to depart from the station, chugging more rapidly as she began to approach a respectable speed.

For Liverpool at least, the daily occurrence of swirling steam across a railway station was consigned to the history books in 1968 when British Rail switched from coal power to diesel, then, in many areas, electrification.

For more than a century Liverpool was at the epi-centre of the steam age. It all began with Stephenson's Rocket at Edge Hill station on September 15, 1830 and the opening of the Liverpool & Manchester railway. And it ended on August 11 1968 at Lime Street when British Rail's last steam train – pulled by Stanier Black 5 Locomotive No. 45110 – chuffed out of the station and into the history books.

memorable movies!

NATIONAL HEADLINES

4 April Dr Martin Luther King is shot dead in the southern US city of Memphis, Tennessee. Dozens of US cities are rocked by race riots.

23 April The first decimal coins make their way into purses throughout Britain, in preparation for replacing pounds, shillings and pence.

3 May The UK's first heart transplant is carried out by a team of 18 doctors and nurses at the National Heart Hospital in Marylebone, London.

10 June Prescription charges are introduced. In the same month, the number of prescriptions in Liverpool dropped by almost 100,000.

11 August The last steam passenger service runs in Britain, making the 314-mile journey from Liverpool to Carlisle.

16 September The General Post Office divides post into first-class and second-class services.

27 September The musical Hair opens in London, one day after the abolition of theatre censorship.

6 November Richard Nixon wins the race to become the next US President.

12 September The Apollo 8 spacecraft becomes the first manned space mission to takes its crew of three safely into orbit around the moon.

Top of the Pops

Crazy World of Arthur Brown – Fire
Louis Armstrong – What A Wonderful World
Rolling Stones (left) – Jumpin' Jack Flash
Mary Hopkin – Those Were The Days
Scaffold – Lily The Pink

Towering above:
St John's Beacon

The high life

Concrete ideas

LIVERPOOL made great strides in taking on a new look in the Sixties.

The quality of life was being celebrated as indisuputedly richer than the previous decade.

There was the redeveloped Pier Head, clean and tidy at last, the eye-catching new St John Beacon, and vital work carried out in the suburbs. Office buildings rose in Old Hall Street or by Lime Street station. Multi-storey homes marked the skyline in Everton and Sheil Park.

And while the cranes lifted a flyover above Dale Street, the same job was being carried out at the city boundary where Queens Drive met Rice lane. The long-awaited second Mersey Tunnel was under construction, and new approach roads made, while West Derby Road was turned into a dual carriageway.

The city's concern for the general raising of standards was seen in the building of a new swimming pool at Speke – the Austin Rawlinson – and the Toxteth Health Centre, Gateacre Comprehensive School and a vast new housing estate at Cantril Farm.

It was not only the 21st century shape of the Metropolitan Cathedral that dramatically altered Liverpool's skyline. Progress was obvious for those who cared to see it; as obvious, definite and solid as the concrete slab swung into place on the side of a new office block.

The beacon-topped Ravenseft development which was changing a vast segment of Liverpool's heart was only one of the city's plans.

The evidence was everywhere that Liverpool's move into the future had already taken place.

A new waterfront view in 1964, with Paddy's Wigwam going up in the background

Left: Kirkby Market with Northwood flats in the background – November 1966

A decade of ups and downs

Streets fall flat for New Towns

THE bulldozed area from which slum houses were cleared represented the real hope of a better life for its former inhabitants.

New flats and maisonettes built in Windsor Street brought patches of green to Toxteth; at Sheil Park, 500 families lived in three new 22-storey blocks, and new homes were built for 39,000 people at Everton. Progress in housing was so rapid that a 14-storey block of flats was regarded as a sensation back in 1961, but easily accepted five years later.

The most vital statistic ever produced in the city was the figure of 3,399 – the record-breaking total of houses and flats built by the Corporation in 1966.

Kirkby, the inspiration behind the popular BBC TV cop programme Z Cars, grew rapidly in the Sixties. The town took in people on Liverpool's housing waiting list and those affected by the slum clearing schemes in the city.

Shops, pubs, parks and gardens, community centres, health centres and clinics were built as well as more than 30 schools, including four comprehensive schools, and a College of Further Education for Kirkby and surrounding district. The eight-storey Civic Building was opened in 1968.

At one time Scotland Road was a centre of cramped terraced homes and a magnet for Irish immigrants, but in the 1960s the bulldozers began to move in and the road would never be the same again. As people moved to homes in the New Towns like Kirkby, Scotland Road changed almost out of recognition. But the memories of that close-knit community will live on forever.

Framed by washing are backyards, kids with an old pram, watched over by Mam and Nan, dominated by the Corporation flats in Fontenoy and Byrom Street

Don't want to go to Kirkby, or Skelmersdale or Speke,
Don't want to go from all we know in Back Buchanan Street..."
Back Buchanan Street, by Harry and Gordon Dison

A world of change: Clockwise from top, William Henry Street 1966 showing the infamous Piggeries; the St John's Market site in 1960 and then nearing completion in 1969; The Walker Art Gallery surrounded by the construction of the Churchill Way flyover in 1968

Memories of the Scottie Road community will live on forever

Gift of the gob

It goes without saying...

THE Scouse accent was simmering in the '60s just like a volcano waiting to erupt onto the wider world.

Liverpool Dockers would give each other nicknames such as Lino (always on the floor) – which would rub off on kids in school playgrounds and the soccer terraces from Goodison to the Kop.

Phrases like Whacker (me feller) and Judy (me bird) were prominent then but are now 'antwacky' (antique).

The stage, radio and television nurtured in the '50s blossomed in the '60s.

The Scouse accent had spread and would spread even further. There were established radio stars like Derek Guyler – a graduate of Tommy Handley's war time show ITMA and later Kenny Everett.

On Television, actor Norman Rossington played Private 'Cupcake' Cook in The Army Game who would dream about his 'scran' (food parcels) sent from his Liverpool family.

Scousisms like Loosie (single ciggy) and Casey (football) were heard on every Mersey ferry and bus to and from the Lanny (Landing) stage.

The Beatles with their natural Scouse accents even convinced some Americans that all Brits spoke like that.

Scouse – the accent may have been officially established in 1890.

But in the '60s it was everywhere, know worra mean, like...

Making the News 1969

STRIKING OUT FOR THE WORKERS

IT was as if things could only go on getting better after the post-war recovery from the mid-1950s, but, along with the greater freedoms and affluence, came terrorism, black-outs, the collapse of much of British industry, strikes, three-day weeks, unemployment, inflation, bombings, and our continuing marginalisation in world affairs.

In Liverpool in the late '60s there were strikes in the docks, followed by stoppages of bus workers, bin workers, construction workers and market porters, creating a climate of resistance in the city. A strike by just 383 women over equal pay paralysed parts of Fords entire operation.

When Barbara Castle, Minister of Transport, officially opened the Mersey Tunnel Approaches Project in 1967, her visit was marked by demonstrations from "locked out" workers at Cammell Laird, who were complaining of 1926 practices at the shipyard.

The Halewood Ford factory suffered its first strike in 1969 when production of 20,000 cars was lost following a walk-out. Employment relations spiralled downwards in February, 1969, as teachers took industrial (in)action when 14 schoolmasters at Holt Comprehensive School, Liverpool, walked out, on the instructions of the National Association of Schoolmasters. This was after Liverpool Education Authority threatened a pay stoppage over the teachers' work to rule in refusing to supervise any voluntary non-teaching activity. It was to herald an era of prolonged unrest in the city.

memorable movies!

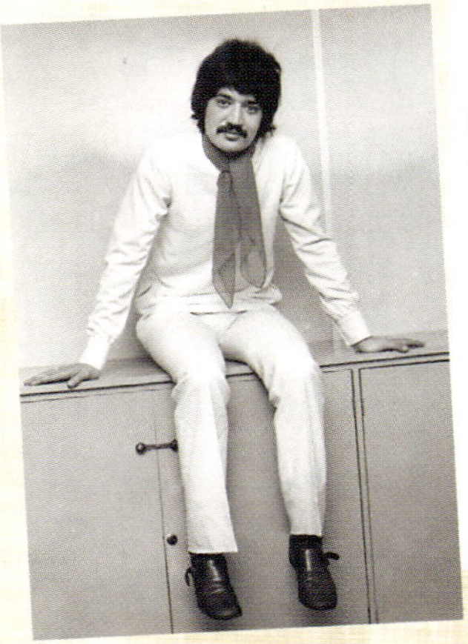

NATIONAL HEADLINES

25 March After their marriage, John Lennon and Yoko Ono celebrate their honeymoon in Amsterdam with a Bed-In to promote world peace.

17 April The Representation of the People Act lowers the voting age in Britain from 22 to 18.

21 July Neil Armstrong becomes the first man to walk on the moon, declaring "That's one small step for man, one giant leap for mankind." The Apollo 11 mission also carried Buzz Aldrin and Michael Collins.

14 August The British Government sends troops into Northern Ireland in what is described as a "limited operation" to restor law and order.

14 October The seven-sided 50p coin comes into circulation to replace the 10-shilling note.

15 November Regular colour television broadcasts begin on BBC1 and ITV.

Top of the Pops

Peter Sarstedt (left) – Where Do You Go To My Lovely

Marvin Gaye (right) – Heard it Through the Grapevine

Archies – Sugar Sugar

The Beatles – The Ballad of John and Yoko

Rolf Harris – Two Little Boys

Other publications from

Trinity Mirror NW²

Wild Merseyside
£4.99+
FREE P+P UK only

Macca, the Saint and the Screen Goddess
£8.99+
Free P+P UK only

Across the Park
£6.99+
Free P+P UK only

Street Stars
£14.99+
Free P+P UK only

Mersey Mastermind
£8.99+
Free P+P UK only

The Great Liverpool Pub Crawl
£8.99+
Free P+P UK only

Talk like the Scousers
£8.99+
Free P+P UK only

Dummy Bullets
£6.99+
Free P+P UK only

Visit www.merseyshop.com or call 0845 143 0001
Monday to Friday 9am-5pm

Trinity Mirror NW²

Trinity Mirror North West & North Wales
PO Box 48, Old Hall Street, Liverpool L69 3EB

Trinity Mirror Sports Media Executive Editor
Ken Rogers

FIRST IN THE SERIES:
LIVERPOOL 50s

In the Sixties, that fab decade of change, we stood at the centre of the world's stage, the old gave way to the new. But the spotlight shifted and the Seventies held a new set of challenges for Merseyside.

NEXT IN THE SERIES:
LIVERPOOL 70s

This is the perfect birthday present or souvenir
for anyone who was born, grew up, or experienced the 1960s in Liverpool. It is also an historic window to the past for anyone wanting to discover what life was like in the area. Packed with unseen images, wonderful memories and nostalgic gems, from the unrivalled archives of the Liverpool Daily Post and Echo, this is a unique collection and record of the decade.

Swing back into the Sixties, the era of Beatlemania, the Ford Anglia and FA Cup glory. From The Cavern to Paddy's Wigwam, from Z-Cars to the Hovercraft, from Subbuteo to Shankly and Catterick – Liverpool was at the centre of a decade that shook the world.

Also available in the series: Liverpool 50s, 70s and 80s.
For more details visit Merseyshop.com or call 0845 143 0001

£4.99
ISBN 978-1-906802-18-9
9 781906 802189

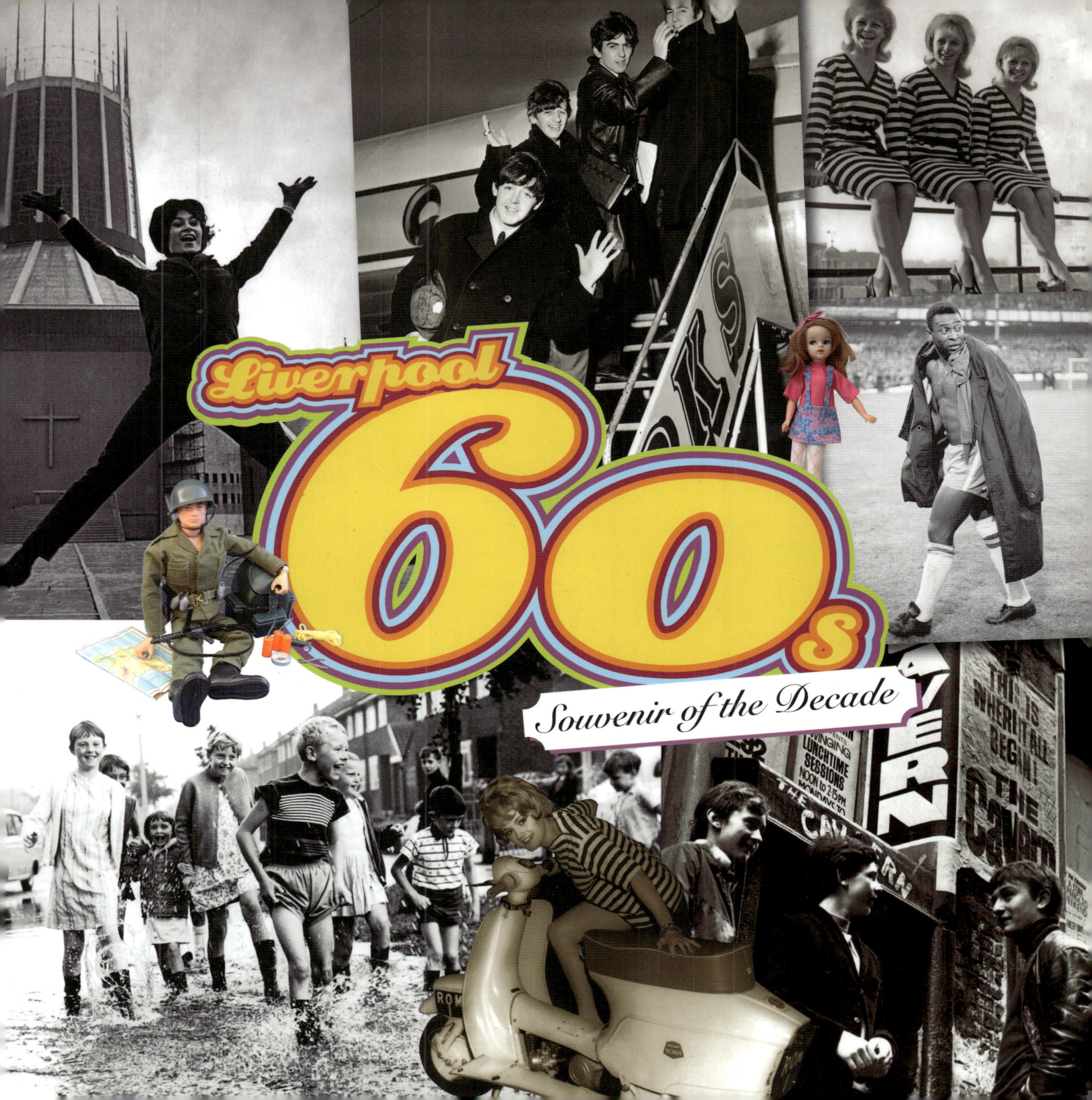
Liverpool
60s
Souvenir of the Decade
LUNCHTIME
SESSIONS
NOON to 2.15PM

A damp winter's morning on the Landing Stage in the early Sixties. The scene could have been 1950, or even 1930, but in 1960 the city stood on the brink of a momentous decade that would change the face and the image of Liverpool for ever